The Tail of Two ~~Two~~ 3 Corgis

at the

DOG SHOW

*by Merlin, Razz and Whimze
with Claudia and Bruce Winkle*

Dog
Show
TODAY

*Illustrated by
Penny Hauffe*

This book is in honor of our *terrific* trainers and handlers.

Terri Greer

Peny Gallogly

Michelle Jackson

Printed in USA
US $16.95

Published by: Merrazz-LLC
All rights reserved   ISBN# 1-978-0-9846868-1-0

First Edition 2013

CPSIA Compliance Information: Batch # 0413
For further CPSIA information contact RJ Communications, NY, NY, 800-621-2556

Merlin is my name.

The dog show ring is my game.

Whimze is my name.
The puppy show ring is my game.

We are Cardigan Welsh Corgi show dogs.
We compete in breed conformation and rally obedience.
We are...

Merlin,

and Whimze,

In conformation, we are judged against our breed standards.
It's just like a beauty contest...

Cardigan Welsh Corgi

.Ability to Move
.Appearance
.Coats
.Coloring

Breed Standards

.Personality
.Size
.Structure
.Temperament

except we don't have to wear swimsuits.

Rally is a sport where we are scored on our skill as we follow the course.

Practicing

my moves...

PUPPY RULES

- *Must be between 4 months and 12 months old.*

- *Must be accompanied by your owner or handler.*

- *Must be nice to others.*

- *Must wait your turn.*

- *Must be quiet.*

- *Must follow the directions of the judge.*

Rub a dub, dub, dub!

Before we go and show,

We are three Corgis in the tub.

Rub a dub. dub, dub!

Razzaberry

Razz

for me!

Strawberry for me!

And then we dry...and dry...and dry
our double coats of fur.

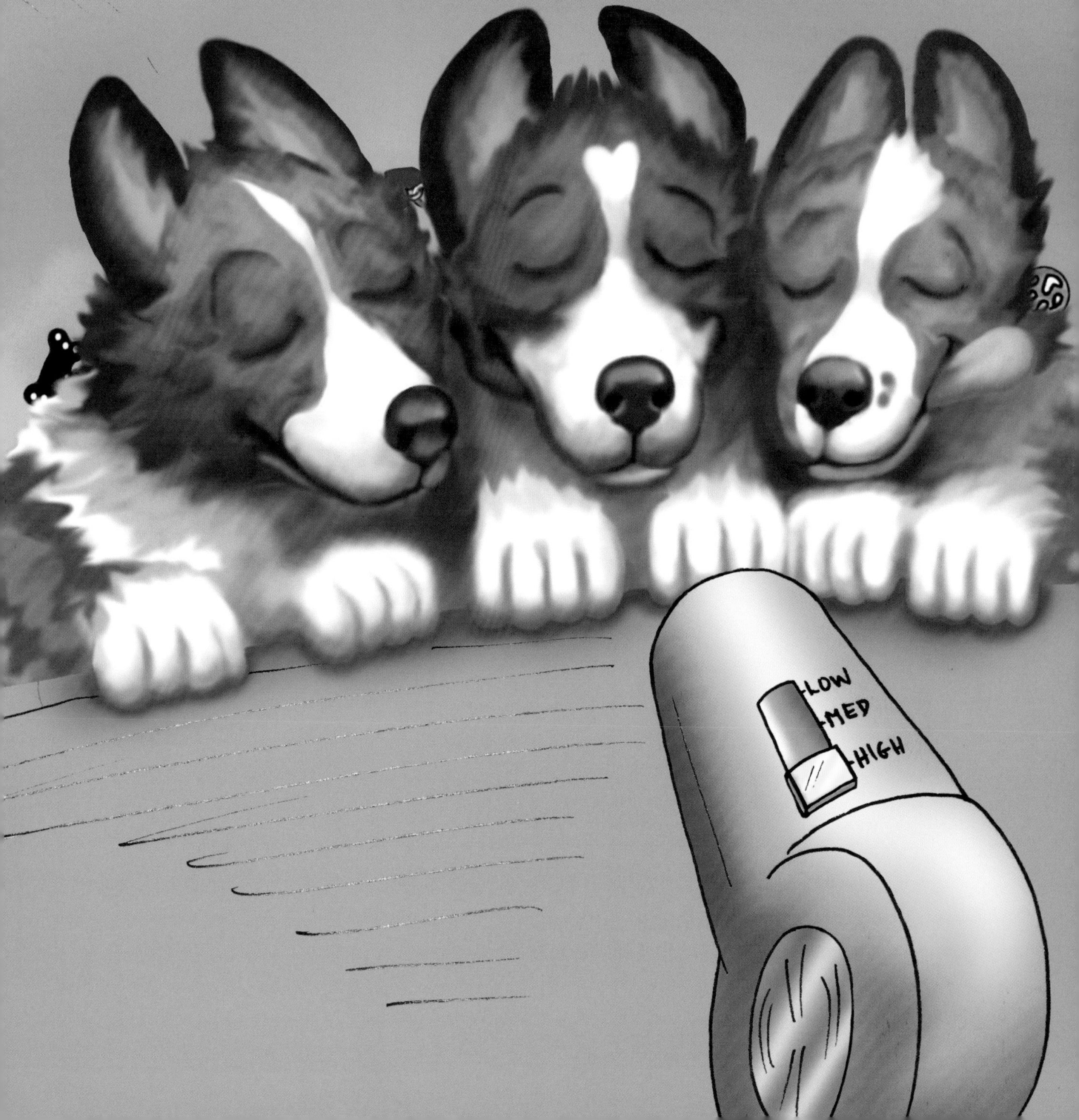

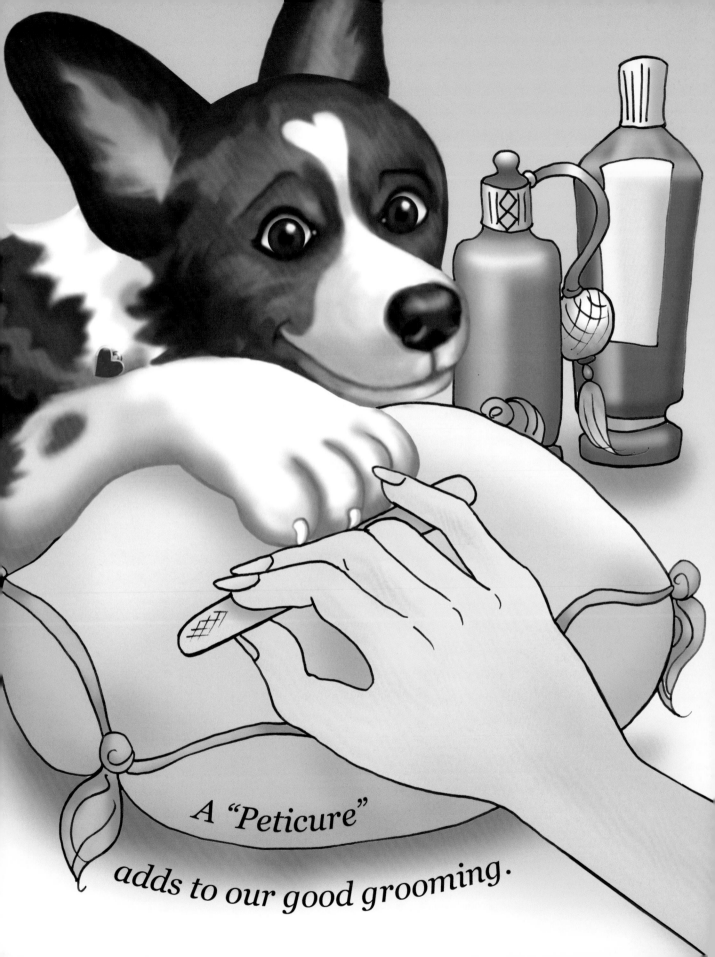

A "Peticure" adds to our good grooming.

or three...

or two

to win a ribbon

It's almost time to show.

Let's go find our rings.

It's my day!

I just won Best of Breed.

I earned a perfect score,

First Place

Second Place

Third Place

and placed Second in my rally competition.
Doggone! First Place beat me by a few seconds.

Watch me strut my stuff.

Oh Boy! Oh Boy! I just won **Best Puppy!**

We finished showing,
and now we're going shopping.

We're tired! On our way home
we dream of all the ribbons
we will win at our next
dog show.

Happiness *is a*
Cardigan Welsh
CORGI

I am an AKC registered Cardigan Welsh Corgi. Officially my name is "Dobcarr's The Magician".

My friends call me **Merlin.**

So far I have won 78 ribbons and Best of Breed 4 times. When I get a few more points I will be an AKC Champion.

Be sure to check out our first book: ***"The Tail of Two Corgis"*** By Merlin and Razz at www.Merrazz-LLC.com or www.Amazon.com

I am an AKC registered Cardigan Welsh Corgi. My Official name is "Dobcarr's Razzamatazz RN".

Everyone calls me **Razz.**

I have earned my Rally Novice title (which is the RN after my name).

Now, I am working towards my Rally Advanced title, which I perform off leash.

Check out our website **www.merrazz-LLC.com** and see the links to our **You Tube Videos.**

I am an AKC
registered Cardigan
Welsh Corgi.
My name is officially
Woodrose
   Acting On A Whim".

You can call me
Whimze.

I am new to the
show ring and
have won 34
ribbons including
Best Puppy,
Best of Breed and
several Best of
Winners.

Be sure to like us
on **FaceBook.**

Claudia, our Mom, has a magnet on her car that says "Cardi Cab" so everyone knows how much she loves us. Mom has to travel a lot for her work, but as soon as she gets home we chase her all around the house. It's our favorite game. Mom encouraged us to write this book too. (It's the second in our series!)

Bruce, our Dad, helps us decide which shows to enter and then helps us get ready to compete. He is quite a sight after he has washed 3 Corgis in the tub, Rub a dub, dub, dub! After we finish showing, he is always there to give us lots of hugs. Now, Merlin is teaching Dad how to be a handler in the breed show ring.

Penny, our very special artist friend, is fun to work with. She comes to our house and sits in the middle of the floor where we all get to play with her. She really has a gift of bringing our true story to life with her magical illustrations. Please check out her wonderful website: www.pennypaint.com

A special thanks to: Laura Lacroix-Johnson for her fabulous photos, Peny Gallogly for her editing reviews and Phil Whitmarsh for his professional printing guidance.